Classic Chocolate Mousse Cake Recipe

Ingredients:

- 1 1/2 cups chocolate cookie crumbs
- 1/4 cup unsalted butter, melted
- 1 1/2 cups semi-sweet chocolate chips
- 1/2 cup hot water
- 2 cups heavy cream, divided
- 3 large eggs, separated
- 1/4 cup granulated sugar
- 1 teaspoon vanilla extract
- 1/4 teaspoon salt

Instructions:

1. PREPARE THE CRUST:

1. Preheat your oven to 350°F (175°C).
2. In a bowl, mix together the chocolate cookie crumbs and melted butter until well combined.
3. Press the mixture into the bottom of a 9-inch springform pan.
4. Bake the crust for 8-10 minutes, then remove from the oven and let it cool completely.

2. MAKE THE CHOCOLATE MOUSSE:

1. In a heatproof bowl, combine the semi-sweet chocolate chips and hot water. Let it sit for a minute, then stir until smooth. Let it cool slightly.
2. In a separate bowl, whip 1 cup of heavy cream until stiff peaks form. Set aside.
3. In another bowl, beat the egg yolks with granulated sugar until thick and pale yellow in color. Stir in the vanilla extract.
4. Gradually stir the melted chocolate mixture into the egg yolk mixture until well combined.
5. Gently fold the whipped cream into the chocolate mixture until no streaks remain. Set aside.

3. ASSEMBLE THE CAKE:

1. In a clean, dry bowl, beat the egg whites with salt until stiff peaks form.
2. Gently fold the beaten egg whites into the chocolate mousse mixture until evenly combined.
3. Pour the mousse over the cooled crust in the springform pan.
4. Smooth the top with a spatula, then refrigerate the cake for at least 4 hours or until set.

4. SERVE:

1. Once the mousse has set, carefully remove the sides of the springform pan.
2. Whip the remaining 1 cup of heavy cream until stiff peaks form, then spread it over the top of the mousse.
3. Garnish with chocolate shavings or cocoa powder if desired.
4. Slice and serve chilled. Enjoy your Classic Chocolate Mousse Cake!

Decadent Dark Chocolate Truffle Mousse Cake Recipe

- 1 1/2 cups chocolate cookie crumbs
- 1/4 cup unsalted butter, melted
- 2 cups dark chocolate chips
- 1 cup heavy cream, divided
- 3 large eggs, separated
- 1/4 cup granulated sugar
- 1 teaspoon vanilla extract
- 1/4 teaspoon salt
- Additional whipped cream and chocolate shavings for garnish (optional)

1. PREPARE THE CRUST:

1. Preheat your oven to 350°F (175°C).
2. In a bowl, mix together the chocolate cookie crumbs and melted butter until well combined.
3. Press the mixture into the bottom of a 9-inch springform pan.
4. Bake the crust for 8-10 minutes, then remove from the oven and let it cool completely.

2. MAKE THE DARK CHOCOLATE TRUFFLE MOUSSE:

1. In a heatproof bowl, combine the dark chocolate chips and 3/4 cup of heavy cream. Microwave in 30-second intervals, stirring in between, until the chocolate is completely melted and smooth. Let it cool slightly.
2. In a separate bowl, whip the remaining 1/4 cup of heavy cream until stiff peaks form. Set aside.
3. In another bowl, beat the egg yolks with granulated sugar until thick and pale yellow in color. Stir in the vanilla extract.
4. Gradually stir the melted chocolate mixture into the egg yolk mixture until well combined.
5. Gently fold the whipped cream into the chocolate mixture until no streaks remain. Set aside.

3. ASSEMBLE THE CAKE:

1. In a clean, dry bowl, beat the egg whites with salt until stiff peaks form.
2. Gently fold the beaten egg whites into the chocolate truffle mousse mixture until evenly combined.
3. Pour the mousse over the cooled crust in the springform pan.

4. Smooth the top with a spatula, then refrigerate the cake for at least 4 hours or until set.

4. SERVE:

1. Once the mousse has set, carefully remove the sides of the springform pan.
2. Optional: Garnish with additional whipped cream and chocolate shavings.
3. Slice and serve chilled. Enjoy your Decadent Dark Chocolate Truffle Mousse Cake!

Heavenly Hazelnut Chocolate Mousse Cake Recipe

- 1 1/2 cups chocolate cookie crumbs
- 1/4 cup hazelnuts, finely chopped
- 1/4 cup unsalted butter, melted
- 1 1/2 cups hazelnut chocolate spread
- 2 cups heavy cream, divided
- 1/4 cup powdered sugar
- 1 teaspoon vanilla extract
- 1/4 teaspoon salt
- Additional hazelnuts and chocolate curls for garnish (optional)

1. PREPARE THE HAZELNUT COOKIE CRUST:

1. Preheat your oven to 350°F (175°C).
2. In a bowl, mix together the chocolate cookie crumbs, finely chopped hazelnuts, and melted butter until well combined.
3. Press the mixture into the bottom of a 9-inch springform pan.
4. Bake the crust for 8-10 minutes, then remove from the oven and let it cool completely.

2. MAKE THE HAZELNUT CHOCOLATE MOUSSE:

1. In a heatproof bowl, microwave the hazelnut chocolate spread until it's softened and easy to stir.
2. In another bowl, whip 1 cup of heavy cream with powdered sugar and vanilla extract until stiff peaks form. Set aside.
3. Gradually fold the softened hazelnut chocolate spread into the whipped cream until well combined.

3. ASSEMBLE THE CAKE:

1. Pour the hazelnut chocolate mousse over the cooled hazelnut cookie crust in the springform pan.
2. Smooth the top with a spatula and refrigerate the cake for at least 4 hours or until set.

4. SERVE:

1. Once the mousse has set, carefully remove the sides of the springform pan.
2. Optional: Garnish with additional hazelnuts and chocolate curls.
3. Slice and serve chilled. Enjoy your Heavenly Hazelnut Chocolate Mousse Cake!

Sinful Salted Caramel Chocolate Mousse Cake Recipe

Ingredients:

- 1 1/2 cups chocolate cookie crumbs
- 1/4 cup unsalted butter, melted
- 1 1/2 cups semi-sweet chocolate chips
- 1/2 cup hot water
- 2 cups heavy cream, divided
- 3 large eggs, separated
- 1/4 cup granulated sugar
- 1 teaspoon vanilla extract
- 1/4 teaspoon salt
- 1 cup caramel sauce (store-bought or homemade)
- Sea salt flakes for garnish

Instructions:

1. PREPARE THE CRUST:

1. Preheat your oven to 350°F (175°C).
2. In a bowl, mix together the chocolate cookie crumbs and melted butter until well combined.
3. Press the mixture into the bottom of a 9-inch springform pan.

4. Bake the crust for 8-10 minutes, then remove from the oven and let it cool completely.

2. MAKE THE CHOCOLATE MOUSSE:

1. In a heatproof bowl, combine the semi-sweet chocolate chips and hot water. Let it sit for a minute, then stir until smooth. Let it cool slightly.
2. In a separate bowl, whip 1 cup of heavy cream until stiff peaks form. Set aside.
3. In another bowl, beat the egg yolks with granulated sugar until thick and pale yellow in color. Stir in the vanilla extract.
4. Gradually stir the melted chocolate mixture into the egg yolk mixture until well combined.
5. Gently fold the whipped cream into the chocolate mixture until no streaks remain. Set aside.

3. ASSEMBLE THE CAKE:

1. In a clean, dry bowl, beat the egg whites with salt until stiff peaks form.
2. Gently fold the beaten egg whites into the chocolate mousse mixture until evenly combined.
3. Pour half of the chocolate mousse over the cooled crust in the springform pan.

4. Drizzle half of the caramel sauce over the mousse layer.
5. Pour the remaining chocolate mousse over the caramel layer.
6. Drizzle the remaining caramel sauce over the top of the mousse.
7. Smooth the top with a spatula, then refrigerate the cake for at least 4 hours or until set.

4. SERVE:

1. Once the mousse has set, carefully remove the sides of the springform pan.
2. Sprinkle sea salt flakes over the top of the cake for garnish.
3. Slice and serve chilled. Enjoy your Sinful Salted Caramel Chocolate Mousse Cake!

Velvety Chocolate Raspberry Mousse Cake Recipe

Ingredients:

- 1 1/2 cups chocolate cookie crumbs
- 1/4 cup unsalted butter, melted
- 1 1/2 cups semi-sweet chocolate chips
- 1/2 cup hot water
- 2 cups heavy cream, divided
- 3 large eggs, separated
- 1/4 cup granulated sugar
- 1 teaspoon vanilla extract
- 1/4 teaspoon salt
- 1 cup fresh raspberries, plus extra for garnish
- 2 tablespoons raspberry jam
- Chocolate shavings for garnish (optional)

Instructions:

1. PREPARE THE CRUST:

1. Preheat your oven to 350°F (175°C).
2. In a bowl, mix together the chocolate cookie crumbs and melted butter until well combined.
3. Press the mixture into the bottom of a 9-inch springform pan.
4. Bake the crust for 8-10 minutes, then remove from the oven and let it cool completely.

2. MAKE THE CHOCOLATE MOUSSE:

1. In a heatproof bowl, combine the semi-sweet chocolate chips and hot water. Let it sit for a minute, then stir until smooth. Let it cool slightly.
2. In a separate bowl, whip 1 cup of heavy cream until stiff peaks form. Set aside.
3. In another bowl, beat the egg yolks with granulated sugar until thick and pale yellow in color. Stir in the vanilla extract.
4. Gradually stir the melted chocolate mixture into the egg yolk mixture until well combined.
5. Gently fold the whipped cream into the chocolate mixture until no streaks remain. Set aside.

3. PREPARE THE RASPBERRY LAYER:

1. In a blender or food processor, puree the fresh raspberries until smooth.
2. Pass the raspberry puree through a fine-mesh sieve to remove the seeds.
3. In a small saucepan, heat the raspberry puree and raspberry jam over low heat until warmed through.

4. ASSEMBLE THE CAKE:

1. Pour half of the chocolate mousse over the cooled crust in the springform pan.

2. Spread a layer of the raspberry mixture over the mousse.
3. Carefully spread the remaining chocolate mousse over the raspberry layer.
4. Smooth the top with a spatula, then refrigerate the cake for at least 4 hours or until set.

5. SERVE:

1. Once the mousse has set, carefully remove the sides of the springform pan.
2. Garnish the top of the cake with fresh raspberries and chocolate shavings if desired.
3. Slice and serve chilled. Enjoy your Velvety Chocolate Raspberry Mousse Cake!

Luxurious Chocolate Ganache Mousse Cake Recipe

Ingredients:

- 1 1/2 cups chocolate cookie crumbs
- 1/4 cup unsalted butter, melted
- 2 cups semi-sweet chocolate chips
- 1 1/2 cups heavy cream, divided
- 3 large eggs, separated
- 1/4 cup granulated sugar
- 1 teaspoon vanilla extract
- 1/4 teaspoon salt

Instructions:

1. PREPARE THE CRUST:

1. Preheat your oven to 350°F (175°C).
2. In a bowl, mix together the chocolate cookie crumbs and melted butter until well combined.
3. Press the mixture into the bottom of a 9-inch springform pan.
4. Bake the crust for 8-10 minutes, then remove from the oven and let it cool completely.

2. MAKE THE CHOCOLATE GANACHE:

1. In a heatproof bowl, combine the semi-sweet chocolate chips and 1 cup of heavy cream.
2. Place the bowl over a pot of simmering water (double boiler) and stir until the chocolate is melted and the mixture is smooth.
3. Remove from heat and let it cool slightly.

3. MAKE THE CHOCOLATE MOUSSE:

1. In a separate bowl, whip the remaining 1/2 cup of heavy cream until stiff peaks form. Set aside.
2. In another bowl, beat the egg yolks with granulated sugar until thick and pale yellow in color. Stir in the vanilla extract.
3. Gradually stir the cooled chocolate ganache into the egg yolk mixture until well combined.
4. Gently fold the whipped cream into the chocolate mixture until no streaks remain. Set aside.

4. ASSEMBLE THE CAKE:

1. In a clean, dry bowl, beat the egg whites with salt until stiff peaks form.
2. Gently fold the beaten egg whites into the chocolate mousse mixture until evenly combined.
3. Pour the mousse over the cooled crust in the springform pan.

4. Smooth the top with a spatula, then refrigerate the cake for at least 4 hours or until set.

5. SERVE:

1. Once the mousse has set, carefully remove the sides of the springform pan.
2. Slice and serve chilled. Enjoy your Luxurious Chocolate Ganache Mousse Cake!

Elegant Espresso Chocolate Mousse Cake Recipe

- 1 1/2 cups chocolate cookie crumbs
- 1/4 cup unsalted butter, melted
- 2 cups semi-sweet chocolate chips
- 1/2 cup hot water
- 2 tablespoons instant espresso powder
- 2 cups heavy cream, divided
- 3 large eggs, separated
- 1/4 cup granulated sugar
- 1 teaspoon vanilla extract
- 1/4 teaspoon salt
- Chocolate-covered espresso beans for garnish (optional)

Instructions:

1. PREPARE THE CRUST:

1. Preheat your oven to 350°F (175°C).
2. In a bowl, mix together the chocolate cookie crumbs and melted butter until well combined.
3. Press the mixture into the bottom of a 9-inch springform pan.
4. Bake the crust for 8-10 minutes, then remove from the oven and let it cool completely.

2. Make the Espresso Chocolate Mousse:

1. In a small bowl, dissolve the instant espresso powder in the hot water. Set aside to cool.
2. In a heatproof bowl, combine the semi-sweet chocolate chips and 1 cup of heavy cream.
3. Place the bowl over a pot of simmering water (double boiler) and stir until the chocolate is melted and the mixture is smooth.
4. Remove from heat and let it cool slightly.

3. In a separate bowl, whip the remaining 1 cup of heavy cream until stiff peaks form. Set aside.

1. In another bowl, beat the egg yolks with granulated sugar until thick and pale yellow in color. Stir in the vanilla extract.
2. Gradually stir the cooled espresso mixture into the egg yolk mixture until well combined.
3. Gradually stir the melted chocolate mixture into the egg yolk mixture until well combined.
4. Gently fold the whipped cream into the chocolate mixture until no streaks remain. Set aside.

4. Assemble the Cake:

1. In a clean, dry bowl, beat the egg whites with salt until stiff peaks form.
2. Gently fold the beaten egg whites into the chocolate mousse mixture until evenly combined.
3. Pour the mousse over the cooled crust in the springform pan.
4. Smooth the top with a spatula, then refrigerate the cake for at least 4 hours or until set.

5. SERVE:

1. Once the mousse has set, carefully remove the sides of the springform pan.
2. Garnish with chocolate-covered espresso beans if desired.
3. Slice and serve chilled. Enjoy your Elegant Espresso Chocolate Mousse Cake!

Indulgent Chocolate Peanut Butter Mousse Cake Recipe

Ingredients:

- 1 1/2 cups chocolate cookie crumbs
- 1/4 cup unsalted butter, melted
- 2 cups semi-sweet chocolate chips
- 1/2 cup creamy peanut butter
- 1/2 cup hot water
- 2 cups heavy cream, divided
- 3 large eggs, separated
- 1/4 cup granulated sugar
- 1 teaspoon vanilla extract
- 1/4 teaspoon salt
- Crushed peanuts for garnish (optional)

Instructions:

1. PREPARE THE CRUST:

1. Preheat your oven to 350°F (175°C).
2. In a bowl, mix together the chocolate cookie crumbs and melted butter until well combined.
3. Press the mixture into the bottom of a 9-inch springform pan.
4. Bake the crust for 8-10 minutes, then remove from the oven and let it cool completely.

2. Make the Chocolate Peanut Butter Mousse:

1. In a heatproof bowl, combine the semi-sweet chocolate chips, creamy peanut butter, and hot water.
2. Place the bowl over a pot of simmering water (double boiler) and stir until the chocolate and peanut butter are melted and the mixture is smooth.
3. Remove from heat and let it cool slightly.
4. In a separate bowl, whip 1 cup of heavy cream until stiff peaks form. Set aside.
5. In another bowl, beat the egg yolks with granulated sugar until thick and pale yellow in color. Stir in the vanilla extract.
6. Gradually stir the cooled chocolate and peanut butter mixture into the egg yolk mixture until well combined.
7. Gently fold the whipped cream into the chocolate and peanut butter mixture until no streaks remain. Set aside.

3. Assemble the Cake:

1. In a clean, dry bowl, beat the egg whites with salt until stiff peaks form.
2. Gently fold the beaten egg whites into the chocolate peanut butter mousse mixture until evenly combined.

3. Pour the mousse over the cooled crust in the springform pan.
4. Smooth the top with a spatula, then refrigerate the cake for at least 4 hours or until set.

4. SERVE:

1. Once the mousse has set, carefully remove the sides of the springform pan.
2. Garnish with crushed peanuts if desired.
3. Slice and serve chilled. Enjoy your Indulgent Chocolate Peanut Butter Mousse Cake!

Divine Chocolate Mint Mousse Cake Recipe

Ingredients:

Ingredients:

- 1 1/2 cups chocolate cookie crumbs
- 1/4 cup unsalted butter, melted
- 2 cups semi-sweet chocolate chips
- 1/2 cup hot water
- 2 cups heavy cream, divided
- 3 large eggs, separated
- 1/4 cup granulated sugar
- 1 teaspoon peppermint extract
- 1/4 teaspoon salt
- Green food coloring (optional)
- Chocolate shavings or fresh mint leaves for garnish (optional)

Instructions:

1. PREPARE THE CRUST:

1. Preheat your oven to 350°F (175°C).
2. In a bowl, mix together the chocolate cookie crumbs and melted butter until well combined.
3. Press the mixture into the bottom of a 9-inch springform pan.
4. Bake the crust for 8-10 minutes, then remove from the oven and let it cool completely.

2. Make the Chocolate Mint Mousse:

1. In a heatproof bowl, combine the semi-sweet chocolate chips and hot water. Let it sit for a minute, then stir until smooth. Let it cool slightly.
2. In a separate bowl, whip 1 cup of heavy cream until stiff peaks form. Set aside.
3. In another bowl, beat the egg yolks with granulated sugar until thick and pale yellow in color. Stir in the peppermint extract and a few drops of green food coloring if desired.
4. Gradually stir the cooled chocolate mixture into the egg yolk mixture until well combined.
5. Gently fold the whipped cream into the chocolate mixture until no streaks remain. Set aside.

3. Assemble the Cake:

1. In a clean, dry bowl, beat the egg whites with salt until stiff peaks form.
2. Gently fold the beaten egg whites into the chocolate mint mousse mixture until evenly combined.
3. Pour the mousse over the cooled crust in the springform pan.
4. Smooth the top with a spatula, then refrigerate the cake for at least 4 hours or until set.

4. SERVE:

1. Once the mousse has set, carefully remove the sides of the springform pan.
2. Garnish with chocolate shavings or fresh mint leaves if desired.
3. Slice and serve chilled. Enjoy your Divine Chocolate Mint Mousse Cake!

Rich Red Velvet Chocolate Mousse Cake Recipe

Ingredients:

- 1 1/2 cups all-purpose flour
- 1 teaspoon baking soda
- 1/4 teaspoon salt
- 1 cup granulated sugar
- 1/2 cup unsalted butter, softened
- 2 large eggs
- 1 teaspoon vanilla extract
- 1 tablespoon cocoa powder
- 1 cup buttermilk
- 1 tablespoon red food coloring
- 1 tablespoon distilled white vinegar
- 1 teaspoon baking powder
- 2 cups semi-sweet chocolate chips
- 1 1/2 cups heavy cream, divided
- 3 large eggs, separated
- 1/4 cup granulated sugar
- 1 teaspoon vanilla extract

Instructions:

1. PREPARE THE RED VELVET CAKE:

1. Preheat your oven to 350°F (175°C). Grease and flour two 9-inch round cake pans.

2. In a medium bowl, sift together the flour, baking soda, cocoa powder, and salt. Set aside.
3. In a large mixing bowl, cream together the softened butter and sugar until light and fluffy.
4. Beat in the eggs one at a time, then stir in the vanilla extract.
5. In a small bowl, mix together the buttermilk and red food coloring. Add the red buttermilk mixture to the batter and mix well.
6. Combine the vinegar and baking powder in a small bowl, then fold it into the batter until fully incorporated.
7. Divide the batter evenly between the prepared cake pans and smooth the tops with a spatula.
8. Bake in the preheated oven for 25-30 minutes, or until a toothpick inserted into the center comes out clean.
9. Remove the cakes from the oven and let them cool in the pans for 10 minutes before transferring to wire racks to cool completely.

2. MAKE THE CHOCOLATE MOUSSE:

1. In a heatproof bowl, combine the semi-sweet chocolate chips and 1 cup of heavy cream.
2. Place the bowl over a pot of simmering water (double boiler) and stir until the chocolate is melted and the mixture is smooth.
3. Remove from heat and let it cool slightly.

4. In a separate bowl, whip the remaining 1/2 cup of heavy cream until stiff peaks form. Set aside.
5. In another bowl, beat the egg yolks with granulated sugar until thick and pale yellow in color. Stir in the vanilla extract.
6. Gradually stir the melted chocolate mixture into the egg yolk mixture until well combined.
7. Gently fold the whipped cream into the chocolate mixture until no streaks remain. Set aside.

3. ASSEMBLE THE CAKE:

1. Once the red velvet cakes have cooled completely, place one layer on a serving plate or cake stand.
2. Spread a layer of chocolate mousse over the top of the cake layer.
3. Place the second red velvet cake layer on top of the mousse layer.
4. Spread the remaining chocolate mousse over the top and sides of the cake, using a spatula to smooth it out.
5. Refrigerate the cake for at least 4 hours, or until the mousse is set.

4. SERVE:

1. Once the mousse has set, slice and serve the Rich Red Velvet Chocolate Mousse Cake.
2. Enjoy the decadent combination of red velvet cake and chocolate mousse!

Silky Smooth White Chocolate Mousse Cake Recipe

Ingredients:

- 1 1/2 cups chocolate cookie crumbs
- 1/4 cup unsalted butter, melted
- 2 cups white chocolate chips
- 1/2 cup hot water
- 2 cups heavy cream, divided
- 3 large eggs, separated
- 1/4 cup granulated sugar
- 1 teaspoon vanilla extract
- 1/4 teaspoon salt

Instructions:

1. PREPARE THE CRUST:

1. Preheat your oven to 350°F (175°C).
2. In a bowl, mix together the chocolate cookie crumbs and melted butter until well combined.
3. Press the mixture into the bottom of a 9-inch springform pan.
4. Bake the crust for 8-10 minutes, then remove from the oven and let it cool completely.

2. MAKE THE WHITE CHOCOLATE MOUSSE:

1. In a heatproof bowl, combine the white chocolate chips and hot water. Let it sit for a minute, then stir until smooth. Let it cool slightly.
2. In a separate bowl, whip 1 cup of heavy cream until stiff peaks form. Set aside.
3. In another bowl, beat the egg yolks with granulated sugar until thick and pale yellow in color. Stir in the vanilla extract.
4. Gradually stir the cooled white chocolate mixture into the egg yolk mixture until well combined.
5. Gently fold the whipped cream into the white chocolate mixture until no streaks remain. Set aside.

3. ASSEMBLE THE CAKE:

1. In a clean, dry bowl, beat the egg whites with salt until stiff peaks form.
2. Gently fold the beaten egg whites into the white chocolate mousse mixture until evenly combined.
3. Pour the mousse over the cooled crust in the springform pan.
4. Smooth the top with a spatula, then refrigerate the cake for at least 4 hours or until set.

4. SERVE:

1. Once the mousse has set, carefully remove the sides of the springform pan.
2. Slice and serve chilled. Enjoy your Silky Smooth White Chocolate Mousse Cake!

Luscious Chocolate Cherry Mousse Cake Recipe

Ingredients:

- 1 1/2 cups chocolate cookie crumbs
- 1/4 cup unsalted butter, melted
- 2 cups semi-sweet chocolate chips
- 1/2 cup cherry preserves or cherry pie filling
- 1/2 cup heavy cream
- 2 cups heavy cream, divided
- 3 large eggs, separated
- 1/4 cup granulated sugar
- 1 teaspoon vanilla extract
- 1/4 teaspoon salt
- Fresh cherries for garnish (optional)

Instructions:

1. PREPARE THE CRUST:

1. Preheat your oven to 350°F (175°C).
2. In a bowl, mix together the chocolate cookie crumbs and melted butter until well combined.
3. Press the mixture into the bottom of a 9-inch springform pan.
4. Bake the crust for 8-10 minutes, then remove from the oven and let it cool completely.

2. Make the Chocolate Cherry Mousse:

1. In a heatproof bowl, combine the semi-sweet chocolate chips and cherry preserves (or cherry pie filling).
2. In a small saucepan, heat 1/2 cup of heavy cream until just simmering.
3. Pour the hot cream over the chocolate and cherry mixture. Let it sit for a minute, then stir until smooth and well combined. Let it cool slightly.
4. In a separate bowl, whip 1 cup of heavy cream until stiff peaks form. Set aside.
5. In another bowl, beat the egg yolks with granulated sugar until thick and pale yellow in color. Stir in the vanilla extract.
6. Gradually stir the cooled chocolate cherry mixture into the egg yolk mixture until well combined.
7. Gently fold the whipped cream into the chocolate cherry mixture until no streaks remain. Set aside.

3. Assemble the Cake:

1. In a clean, dry bowl, beat the egg whites with salt until stiff peaks form.

2. Gently fold the beaten egg whites into the chocolate cherry mousse mixture until evenly combined.
3. Pour the mousse over the cooled crust in the springform pan.
4. Smooth the top with a spatula, then refrigerate the cake for at least 4 hours or until set.

4. SERVE:

1. Once the mousse has set, carefully remove the sides of the springform pan.
2. Garnish with fresh cherries if desired.
3. Slice and serve chilled. Enjoy your Luscious Chocolate Cherry Mousse Cake!

Blissful Chocolate Almond Mousse Cake Recipe

- 1 1/2 cups chocolate cookie crumbs
- 1/4 cup unsalted butter, melted
- 1 1/2 cups semi-sweet chocolate chips
- 1/2 cup almond butter
- 1/2 cup hot water
- 2 cups heavy cream, divided
- 3 large eggs, separated
- 1/4 cup granulated sugar
- 1 teaspoon almond extract
- 1/4 teaspoon salt
- Sliced almonds for garnish (optional)

Instructions:

1. PREPARE THE CRUST:

1. Preheat your oven to 350°F (175°C).
2. In a bowl, mix together the chocolate cookie crumbs and melted butter until well combined.
3. Press the mixture into the bottom of a 9-inch springform pan.
4. Bake the crust for 8-10 minutes, then remove from the oven and let it cool completely.

2. Make the Chocolate Almond Mousse:

1. In a heatproof bowl, combine the semi-sweet chocolate chips, almond butter, and hot water.
2. Place the bowl over a pot of simmering water (double boiler) and stir until the chocolate and almond butter are melted and the mixture is smooth.
3. Remove from heat and let it cool slightly.
4. In a separate bowl, whip 1 cup of heavy cream until stiff peaks form. Set aside.
5. In another bowl, beat the egg yolks with granulated sugar until thick and pale yellow in color. Stir in the almond extract.
6. Gradually stir the cooled chocolate and almond butter mixture into the egg yolk mixture until well combined.
7. Gently fold the whipped cream into the chocolate almond mixture until no streaks remain. Set aside.

3. Assemble the Cake:

1. In a clean, dry bowl, beat the egg whites with salt until stiff peaks form.
2. Gently fold the beaten egg whites into the chocolate almond mousse mixture until evenly combined.

3. Pour the mousse over the cooled crust in the springform pan.
4. Smooth the top with a spatula, then refrigerate the cake for at least 4 hours or until set.

4. SERVE:

1. Once the mousse has set, carefully remove the sides of the springform pan.
2. Garnish with sliced almonds if desired.
3. Slice and serve chilled. Enjoy your Blissful Chocolate Almond Mousse Cake!

Gourmet Chocolate Macadamia Mousse Cake Recipe

Ingredients:

- 1 1/2 cups chocolate cookie crumbs
- 1/4 cup unsalted butter, melted
- 1 1/2 cups semi-sweet chocolate chips
- 1/2 cup macadamia nuts, chopped
- 1/2 cup heavy cream
- 2 cups heavy cream, divided
- 3 large eggs, separated
- 1/4 cup granulated sugar
- 1 teaspoon vanilla extract
- 1/4 teaspoon salt
- Additional macadamia nuts for garnish (optional)

Instructions:

1. PREPARE THE CRUST:

1. Preheat your oven to 350°F (175°C).
2. In a bowl, mix together the chocolate cookie crumbs, chopped macadamia nuts, and melted butter until well combined.

3. Press the mixture into the bottom of a 9-inch springform pan.
4. Bake the crust for 8-10 minutes, then remove from the oven and let it cool completely.

2. MAKE THE CHOCOLATE MACADAMIA MOUSSE:

1. In a heatproof bowl, combine the semi-sweet chocolate chips and 1/2 cup of heavy cream.
2. Place the bowl over a pot of simmering water (double boiler) and stir until the chocolate is melted and the mixture is smooth.
3. Remove from heat and let it cool slightly.
4. In a separate bowl, whip 1 cup of heavy cream until stiff peaks form. Set aside.
5. In another bowl, beat the egg yolks with granulated sugar until thick and pale yellow in color. Stir in the vanilla extract.
6. Gradually stir the cooled chocolate mixture into the egg yolk mixture until well combined.
7. Gently fold the whipped cream into the chocolate mixture until no streaks remain. Set aside.

3. ASSEMBLE THE CAKE:

1. In a clean, dry bowl, beat the egg whites with salt until stiff peaks form.

2. Gently fold the beaten egg whites into the chocolate mousse mixture until evenly combined.
3. Pour the mousse over the cooled crust in the springform pan.
4. Smooth the top with a spatula, then refrigerate the cake for at least 4 hours or until set.

4. SERVE:

1. Once the mousse has set, carefully remove the sides of the springform pan.
2. Garnish with additional chopped macadamia nuts if desired.
3. Slice and serve chilled. Enjoy your Gourmet Chocolate Macadamia Mousse Cake!

Dreamy Chocolate Coconut Mousse Cake Recipe

Ingredients:

- 1 1/2 cups chocolate cookie crumbs
- 1/4 cup unsalted butter, melted
- 1 1/2 cups semi-sweet chocolate chips
- 1 cup coconut cream
- 1/2 cup shredded coconut, toasted
- 2 cups heavy cream, divided
- 3 large eggs, separated
- 1/4 cup granulated sugar
- 1 teaspoon vanilla extract
- 1/4 teaspoon salt
- Additional shredded coconut for garnish (optional)

Instructions:

1. PREPARE THE CRUST:

1. Preheat your oven to 350°F (175°C).
2. In a bowl, mix together the chocolate cookie crumbs, toasted shredded coconut, and melted butter until well combined.
3. Press the mixture into the bottom of a 9-inch springform pan.

4. Bake the crust for 8-10 minutes, then remove from the oven and let it cool completely.

2. MAKE THE CHOCOLATE COCONUT MOUSSE:

1. In a heatproof bowl, combine the semi-sweet chocolate chips and coconut cream.
2. Place the bowl over a pot of simmering water (double boiler) and stir until the chocolate is melted and the mixture is smooth.
3. Remove from heat and let it cool slightly.
4. In a separate bowl, whip 1 cup of heavy cream until stiff peaks form. Set aside.
5. In another bowl, beat the egg yolks with granulated sugar until thick and pale yellow in color. Stir in the vanilla extract.
6. Gradually stir the cooled chocolate mixture into the egg yolk mixture until well combined.
7. Gently fold the whipped cream into the chocolate mixture until no streaks remain. Set aside.

3. ASSEMBLE THE CAKE:

1. In a clean, dry bowl, beat the egg whites with salt until stiff peaks form.
2. Gently fold the beaten egg whites into the chocolate coconut mousse mixture until evenly combined.

3. Pour the mousse over the cooled crust in the springform pan.
4. Smooth the top with a spatula, then refrigerate the cake for at least 4 hours or until set.

4. SERVE:

1. Once the mousse has set, carefully remove the sides of the springform pan.
2. Garnish with additional shredded coconut if desired.
3. Slice and serve chilled. Enjoy your Dreamy Chocolate Coconut Mousse Cake!

Delicate Chocolate Rose Mousse Cake Recipe

- 1 1/2 cups chocolate cookie crumbs
- 1/4 cup unsalted butter, melted
- 2 cups semi-sweet chocolate chips
- 1/2 cup rose water
- 2 cups heavy cream, divided
- 3 large eggs, separated
- 1/4 cup granulated sugar
- 1 teaspoon vanilla extract
- 1/4 teaspoon salt
- Edible rose petals for garnish (optional)

1. PREPARE THE CRUST:

1. Preheat your oven to 350°F (175°C).
2. In a bowl, mix together the chocolate cookie crumbs and melted butter until well combined.
3. Press the mixture into the bottom of a 9-inch springform pan.
4. Bake the crust for 8-10 minutes, then remove from the oven and let it cool completely.

2. MAKE THE CHOCOLATE ROSE MOUSSE:

1. In a heatproof bowl, combine the semi-sweet chocolate chips and rose water.
2. In a small saucepan, heat 1/2 cup of heavy cream until just simmering.
3. Pour the hot cream over the chocolate and rose water mixture. Let it sit for a minute, then stir until smooth and well combined. Let it cool slightly.
4. In a separate bowl, whip 1 cup of heavy cream until stiff peaks form. Set aside.
5. In another bowl, beat the egg yolks with granulated sugar until thick and pale yellow in color. Stir in the vanilla extract.
6. Gradually stir the cooled chocolate rose mixture into the egg yolk mixture until well combined.
7. Gently fold the whipped cream into the chocolate rose mixture until no streaks remain. Set aside.

3. ASSEMBLE THE CAKE:

1. In a clean, dry bowl, beat the egg whites with salt until stiff peaks form.
2. Gently fold the beaten egg whites into the chocolate rose mousse mixture until evenly combined.
3. Pour the mousse over the cooled crust in the springform pan.

4. Smooth the top with a spatula, then refrigerate the cake for at least 4 hours or until set.

4. SERVE:

1. Once the mousse has set, carefully remove the sides of the springform pan.
2. Garnish with edible rose petals if desired.
3. Slice and serve chilled. Enjoy your Delicate Chocolate Rose Mousse Cake!

Exquisite Chocolate Bourbon Mousse Cake Recipe

Ingredients:

- 1 1/2 cups chocolate cookie crumbs
- 1/4 cup unsalted butter, melted
- 2 cups semi-sweet chocolate chips
- 1/4 cup bourbon
- 2 cups heavy cream, divided
- 3 large eggs, separated
- 1/4 cup granulated sugar
- 1 teaspoon vanilla extract
- 1/4 teaspoon salt
- Whipped cream and chocolate shavings for garnish (optional)

Instructions:

1. PREPARE THE CRUST:

1. Preheat your oven to 350°F (175°C).
2. In a bowl, mix together the chocolate cookie crumbs and melted butter until well combined.
3. Press the mixture into the bottom of a 9-inch springform pan.
4. Bake the crust for 8-10 minutes, then remove from the oven and let it cool completely.

2. MAKE THE CHOCOLATE BOURBON MOUSSE:

1. In a heatproof bowl, combine the semi-sweet chocolate chips and bourbon.
2. In a small saucepan, heat 1/2 cup of heavy cream until just simmering.
3. Pour the hot cream over the chocolate and bourbon mixture. Let it sit for a minute, then stir until smooth and well combined. Let it cool slightly.
4. In a separate bowl, whip 1 cup of heavy cream until stiff peaks form. Set aside.
5. In another bowl, beat the egg yolks with granulated sugar until thick and pale yellow in color. Stir in the vanilla extract.
6. Gradually stir the cooled chocolate bourbon mixture into the egg yolk mixture until well combined.
7. Gently fold the whipped cream into the chocolate bourbon mixture until no streaks remain. Set aside.

3. ASSEMBLE THE CAKE:

1. In a clean, dry bowl, beat the egg whites with salt until stiff peaks form.
2. Gently fold the beaten egg whites into the chocolate bourbon mousse mixture until evenly combined.

3. Pour the mousse over the cooled crust in the springform pan.
4. Smooth the top with a spatula, then refrigerate the cake for at least 4 hours or until set.

4. SERVE:

1. Once the mousse has set, carefully remove the sides of the springform pan.
2. Garnish with whipped cream and chocolate shavings if desired.
3. Slice and serve chilled. Enjoy your Exquisite Chocolate Bourbon Mousse Cake!

Sophisticated Chocolate Pistachio Mousse Cake Recipe

- 1 1/2 cups chocolate cookie crumbs
- 1/4 cup unsalted butter, melted
- 2 cups semi-sweet chocolate chips
- 1 cup shelled pistachios, finely ground
- 1/2 cup heavy cream
- 2 cups heavy cream, divided
- 3 large eggs, separated
- 1/4 cup granulated sugar
- 1 teaspoon vanilla extract
- 1/4 teaspoon salt
- Additional chopped pistachios for garnish (optional)

1. PREPARE THE CRUST:

1. Preheat your oven to 350°F (175°C).
2. In a bowl, mix together the chocolate cookie crumbs, finely ground pistachios, and melted butter until well combined.
3. Press the mixture into the bottom of a 9-inch springform pan.

4. Bake the crust for 8-10 minutes, then remove from the oven and let it cool completely.

2. MAKE THE CHOCOLATE PISTACHIO MOUSSE:

1. In a heatproof bowl, combine the semi-sweet chocolate chips and 1/2 cup of heavy cream.
2. Place the bowl over a pot of simmering water (double boiler) and stir until the chocolate is melted and the mixture is smooth.
3. Remove from heat and let it cool slightly.
4. In a separate bowl, whip 1 cup of heavy cream until stiff peaks form. Set aside.
5. In another bowl, beat the egg yolks with granulated sugar until thick and pale yellow in color. Stir in the vanilla extract.
6. Gradually stir the cooled chocolate mixture into the egg yolk mixture until well combined.
7. Gently fold the whipped cream into the chocolate mixture until no streaks remain. Set aside.

3. ASSEMBLE THE CAKE:

1. In a clean, dry bowl, beat the egg whites with salt until stiff peaks form.
2. Gently fold the beaten egg whites into the chocolate pistachio mousse mixture until evenly combined.

3. Pour the mousse over the cooled crust in the springform pan.
4. Smooth the top with a spatula, then refrigerate the cake for at least 4 hours or until set.

4. SERVE:

1. Once the mousse has set, carefully remove the sides of the springform pan.
2. Garnish with additional chopped pistachios if desired.
3. Slice and serve chilled. Enjoy your Sophisticated Chocolate Pistachio Mousse Cake!

Irresistible Chocolate Banana Mousse Cake Recipe

Ingredients:

- 1 1/2 cups chocolate cookie crumbs
- 1/4 cup unsalted butter, melted
- 2 ripe bananas, mashed
- 2 cups semi-sweet chocolate chips
- 1/2 cup heavy cream
- 2 cups heavy cream, divided
- 3 large eggs, separated
- 1/4 cup granulated sugar
- 1 teaspoon vanilla extract
- 1/4 teaspoon salt
- Sliced bananas and chocolate curls for garnish (optional)

Instructions:

1. PREPARE THE CRUST:

1. Preheat your oven to 350°F (175°C).
2. In a bowl, mix together the chocolate cookie crumbs and melted butter until well combined.
3. Press the mixture into the bottom of a 9-inch springform pan.
4. Bake the crust for 8-10 minutes, then remove from the oven and let it cool completely.

2. MAKE THE CHOCOLATE BANANA MOUSSE:

1. In a heatproof bowl, combine the semi-sweet chocolate chips and mashed bananas.
2. In a small saucepan, heat 1/2 cup of heavy cream until just simmering.
3. Pour the hot cream over the chocolate and banana mixture. Let it sit for a minute, then stir until smooth and well combined. Let it cool slightly.
4. In a separate bowl, whip 1 cup of heavy cream until stiff peaks form. Set aside.
5. In another bowl, beat the egg yolks with granulated sugar until thick and pale yellow in color. Stir in the vanilla extract.
6. Gradually stir the cooled chocolate banana mixture into the egg yolk mixture until well combined.
7. Gently fold the whipped cream into the chocolate banana mixture until no streaks remain. Set aside.

3. ASSEMBLE THE CAKE:

1. In a clean, dry bowl, beat the egg whites with salt until stiff peaks form.
2. Gently fold the beaten egg whites into the chocolate banana mousse mixture until evenly combined.

3. Pour the mousse over the cooled crust in the springform pan.
4. Smooth the top with a spatula, then refrigerate the cake for at least 4 hours or until set.

4. SERVE:

1. Once the mousse has set, carefully remove the sides of the springform pan.
2. Garnish with sliced bananas and chocolate curls if desired.
3. Slice and serve chilled. Enjoy your Irresistible Chocolate Banana Mousse Cake!

Heavenly Chocolate Lavender Mousse Cake Recipe

- 1 1/2 cups chocolate cookie crumbs
- 1/4 cup unsalted butter, melted
- 2 cups semi-sweet chocolate chips
- 1 tablespoon dried culinary lavender
- 1 cup heavy cream
- 2 cups heavy cream, divided
- 3 large eggs, separated
- 1/4 cup granulated sugar
- 1 teaspoon vanilla extract
- 1/4 teaspoon salt
- Lavender flowers for garnish (optional)

1. PREPARE THE CRUST:

1. Preheat your oven to 350°F (175°C).
2. In a bowl, mix together the chocolate cookie crumbs and melted butter until well combined.
3. Press the mixture into the bottom of a 9-inch springform pan.
4. Bake the crust for 8-10 minutes, then remove from the oven and let it cool completely.

2. Infuse the Chocolate with Lavender:

1. In a small saucepan, heat 1 cup of heavy cream over medium heat until it just begins to simmer.
2. Remove the cream from heat and add the dried lavender. Let it steep for 10-15 minutes.
3. Strain the cream through a fine-mesh sieve to remove the lavender. Set aside.

3. Make the Lavender Chocolate Mousse:

1. In a heatproof bowl, combine the semi-sweet chocolate chips and infused cream.
2. Place the bowl over a pot of simmering water (double boiler) and stir until the chocolate is melted and the mixture is smooth.
3. Remove from heat and let it cool slightly.
4. In a separate bowl, whip 1 cup of heavy cream until stiff peaks form. Set aside.
5. In another bowl, beat the egg yolks with granulated sugar until thick and pale yellow in color. Stir in the vanilla extract.
6. Gradually stir the cooled lavender chocolate mixture into the egg yolk mixture until well combined.

7. Gently fold the whipped cream into the chocolate mixture until no streaks remain. Set aside.

4. ASSEMBLE THE CAKE:

1. In a clean, dry bowl, beat the egg whites with salt until stiff peaks form.
2. Gently fold the beaten egg whites into the lavender chocolate mousse mixture until evenly combined.
3. Pour the mousse over the cooled crust in the springform pan.
4. Smooth the top with a spatula, then refrigerate the cake for at least 4 hours or until set.

5. SERVE:

1. Once the mousse has set, carefully remove the sides of the springform pan.
2. Garnish with lavender flowers if desired.
3. Slice and serve chilled. Enjoy your Heavenly Chocolate Lavender Mousse Cake!

Velvety Chocolate Avocado Mousse Cake Recipe

Ingredients:

- 1 1/2 cups chocolate cookie crumbs
- 1/4 cup unsalted butter, melted
- 2 ripe avocados, peeled and pitted
- 1/2 cup cocoa powder
- 1/2 cup maple syrup or honey
- 1 teaspoon vanilla extract
- Pinch of salt
- 2 cups heavy cream, divided
- 1/4 cup powdered sugar
- Chocolate shavings or cocoa powder for garnish (optional)

Instructions:

1. PREPARE THE CRUST:

1. Preheat your oven to 350°F (175°C).
2. In a bowl, mix together the chocolate cookie crumbs and melted butter until well combined.
3. Press the mixture into the bottom of a 9-inch springform pan.
4. Bake the crust for 8-10 minutes, then remove from the oven and let it cool completely.

2. Make the Chocolate Avocado Mousse:

1. In a food processor or blender, combine the ripe avocados, cocoa powder, maple syrup (or honey), vanilla extract, and a pinch of salt. Blend until smooth and creamy.
2. In a separate bowl, whip 1 cup of heavy cream until stiff peaks form.
3. Gently fold the avocado-chocolate mixture into the whipped cream until well combined and no streaks remain.

3. Assemble the Cake:

1. Pour the chocolate avocado mousse over the cooled crust in the springform pan.
2. Smooth the top with a spatula, then refrigerate the cake for at least 4 hours or until set.

4. Make the Whipped Cream Topping:

1. In a chilled bowl, whip the remaining 1 cup of heavy cream with powdered sugar until stiff peaks form.

5. Serve:

1. Once the mousse has set, carefully remove the sides of the springform pan.

2. Spread the whipped cream over the top of the mousse cake.
3. Garnish with chocolate shavings or a dusting of cocoa powder if desired.
4. Slice and serve chilled. Enjoy your Velvety Chocolate Avocado Mousse Cake!

Silky Chocolate Chai Mousse Cake Recipe

Ingredients:

- 1 1/2 cups chocolate cookie crumbs
- 1/4 cup unsalted butter, melted
- 2 cups semi-sweet chocolate chips
- 2 chai tea bags
- 1/2 cup heavy cream
- 2 cups heavy cream, divided
- 3 large eggs, separated
- 1/4 cup granulated sugar
- 1 teaspoon vanilla extract
- 1/4 teaspoon ground cinnamon
- 1/4 teaspoon ground ginger
- 1/4 teaspoon ground cardamom
- 1/4 teaspoon ground cloves
- 1/4 teaspoon ground nutmeg

Instructions:

1. PREPARE THE CRUST:

1. Preheat your oven to 350°F (175°C).
2. In a bowl, mix together the chocolate cookie crumbs and melted butter until well combined.
3. Press the mixture into the bottom of a 9-inch springform pan.

4. Bake the crust for 8-10 minutes, then remove from the oven and let it cool completely.

2. INFUSE THE CHOCOLATE WITH CHAI:

1. In a small saucepan, heat 1/2 cup of heavy cream over medium heat until it just begins to simmer.
2. Remove the cream from heat and add the chai tea bags. Let them steep for 10-15 minutes.
3. Remove the tea bags and gently squeeze out any excess liquid. Set aside.

3. MAKE THE CHAI CHOCOLATE MOUSSE:

1. In a heatproof bowl, combine the semi-sweet chocolate chips and infused cream.
2. Place the bowl over a pot of simmering water (double boiler) and stir until the chocolate is melted and the mixture is smooth.
3. Remove from heat and let it cool slightly.
4. In a separate bowl, whip 1 cup of heavy cream until stiff peaks form. Set aside.
5. In another bowl, beat the egg yolks with granulated sugar until thick and pale yellow in color. Stir in the vanilla extract and spices (cinnamon, ginger, cardamom, cloves, nutmeg).

6. Gradually stir the cooled chai chocolate mixture into the egg yolk mixture until well combined.
7. Gently fold the whipped cream into the chocolate mixture until no streaks remain. Set aside.

4. ASSEMBLE THE CAKE:

1. In a clean, dry bowl, beat the egg whites with a pinch of salt until stiff peaks form.
2. Gently fold the beaten egg whites into the chai chocolate mousse mixture until evenly combined.
3. Pour the mousse over the cooled crust in the springform pan.
4. Smooth the top with a spatula, then refrigerate the cake for at least 4 hours or until set.

5. SERVE:

1. Once the mousse has set, carefully remove the sides of the springform pan.
2. Slice and serve chilled. Enjoy your Silky Chocolate Chai Mousse Cake!

Elegant Chocolate Cardamom Mousse Cake Recipe

- 1 1/2 cups chocolate cookie crumbs
- 1/4 cup unsalted butter, melted
- 2 cups semi-sweet chocolate chips
- 1 teaspoon ground cardamom
- 1/2 cup heavy cream
- 2 cups heavy cream, divided
- 3 large eggs, separated
- 1/4 cup granulated sugar
- 1 teaspoon vanilla extract
- 1/4 teaspoon salt
- Additional chocolate shavings or cocoa powder for garnish (optional)

1. PREPARE THE CRUST:

1. Preheat your oven to 350°F (175°C).
2. In a bowl, mix together the chocolate cookie crumbs and melted butter until well combined.
3. Press the mixture into the bottom of a 9-inch springform pan.
4. Bake the crust for 8-10 minutes, then remove from the oven and let it cool completely.

2. MAKE THE CARDAMOM CHOCOLATE MOUSSE:

1. In a heatproof bowl, combine the semi-sweet chocolate chips and ground cardamom.
2. In a small saucepan, heat 1/2 cup of heavy cream until just simmering.
3. Pour the hot cream over the chocolate and cardamom mixture. Let it sit for a minute, then stir until smooth and well combined. Let it cool slightly.
4. In a separate bowl, whip 1 cup of heavy cream until stiff peaks form. Set aside.
5. In another bowl, beat the egg yolks with granulated sugar until thick and pale yellow in color. Stir in the vanilla extract.
6. Gradually stir the cooled chocolate cardamom mixture into the egg yolk mixture until well combined.
7. Gently fold the whipped cream into the chocolate cardamom mixture until no streaks remain. Set aside.

3. ASSEMBLE THE CAKE:

1. In a clean, dry bowl, beat the egg whites with salt until stiff peaks form.
2. Gently fold the beaten egg whites into the chocolate cardamom mousse mixture until evenly combined.

3. Pour the mousse over the cooled crust in the springform pan.
4. Smooth the top with a spatula, then refrigerate the cake for at least 4 hours or until set.

4. SERVE:

1. Once the mousse has set, carefully remove the sides of the springform pan.
2. Garnish with chocolate shavings or dust with cocoa powder if desired.
3. Slice and serve chilled. Enjoy your Elegant Chocolate Cardamom Mousse Cake!

Rich Chocolate Red Wine Mousse Cake Recipe

Ingredients:

- 1 1/2 cups chocolate cookie crumbs
- 1/4 cup unsalted butter, melted
- 2 cups semi-sweet chocolate chips
- 1/2 cup red wine (choose a full-bodied red wine like Merlot or Cabernet Sauvignon)
- 1/2 cup heavy cream
- 2 cups heavy cream, divided
- 3 large eggs, separated
- 1/4 cup granulated sugar
- 1 teaspoon vanilla extract
- 1/4 teaspoon salt
- Additional whipped cream and chocolate shavings for garnish (optional)

Instructions:

1. PREPARE THE CRUST:

1. Preheat your oven to 350°F (175°C).
2. In a bowl, mix together the chocolate cookie crumbs and melted butter until well combined.
3. Press the mixture into the bottom of a 9-inch springform pan.

4. Bake the crust for 8-10 minutes, then remove from the oven and let it cool completely.

2. MAKE THE RED WINE CHOCOLATE MOUSSE:

1. In a small saucepan, heat the red wine over medium heat until it just begins to simmer. Let it reduce by half.
2. Remove the reduced wine from heat and let it cool slightly.
3. In a heatproof bowl, combine the semi-sweet chocolate chips and reduced red wine.
4. Place the bowl over a pot of simmering water (double boiler) and stir until the chocolate is melted and the mixture is smooth.
5. Remove from heat and let it cool slightly.
6. In a separate bowl, whip 1 cup of heavy cream until stiff peaks form. Set aside.
7. In another bowl, beat the egg yolks with granulated sugar until thick and pale yellow in color. Stir in the vanilla extract.
8. Gradually stir the cooled chocolate red wine mixture into the egg yolk mixture until well combined.
9. Gently fold the whipped cream into the chocolate red wine mixture until no streaks remain. Set aside.

3. ASSEMBLE THE CAKE:

1. In a clean, dry bowl, beat the egg whites with salt until stiff peaks form.
2. Gently fold the beaten egg whites into the chocolate red wine mousse mixture until evenly combined.
3. Pour the mousse over the cooled crust in the springform pan.
4. Smooth the top with a spatula, then refrigerate the cake for at least 4 hours or until set.

4. SERVE:

1. Once the mousse has set, carefully remove the sides of the springform pan.
2. Garnish with whipped cream and chocolate shavings if desired.
3. Slice and serve chilled. Enjoy your Rich Chocolate Red Wine Mousse Cake!

Divine Chocolate Strawberry Mousse Cake Recipe

Ingredients:

- 1 1/2 cups chocolate cookie crumbs
- 1/4 cup unsalted butter, melted
- 2 cups semi-sweet chocolate chips
- 1 cup heavy cream
- 2 cups heavy cream, divided
- 1/4 cup granulated sugar
- 1 teaspoon vanilla extract
- 1/4 teaspoon salt
- 1 cup fresh strawberries, chopped
- Extra fresh strawberries for garnish (optional)

Instructions:

1. PREPARE THE CRUST:

1. Preheat the oven to 350°F (175°C).
2. In a bowl, mix together the chocolate cookie crumbs and melted butter until well combined.
3. Press the mixture into the bottom of a 9-inch springform pan to form the crust.
4. Bake the crust for 8-10 minutes, then remove from the oven and let it cool completely.

2. MAKE THE CHOCOLATE MOUSSE:

1. In a small saucepan, heat 1 cup of heavy cream over medium heat until it's just simmering.
2. Remove from heat and add the semi-sweet chocolate chips. Stir until melted and smooth.
3. In a separate bowl, whip 1 cup of heavy cream until stiff peaks form.
4. In another bowl, beat the egg yolks with granulated sugar until pale and fluffy. Mix in the vanilla extract.
5. Gradually fold the melted chocolate mixture into the egg yolk mixture.
6. Gently fold in the whipped cream until no streaks remain.

3. ASSEMBLE THE CAKE:

1. Spread a layer of chopped strawberries over the cooled crust.
2. Pour the chocolate mousse over the strawberries and smooth the top with a spatula.
3. Refrigerate the cake for at least 4 hours or until set.

4. SERVE:

1. Once set, remove the cake from the springform pan.
2. Garnish with additional fresh strawberries if desired.

3. Slice and serve chilled. Enjoy your Divine Chocolate Strawberry Mousse Cake!

Sinful Chocolate Mocha Mousse Cake Recipe

- 1 1/2 cups chocolate cookie crumbs
- 1/4 cup unsalted butter, melted
- 2 cups semi-sweet chocolate chips
- 1 tablespoon instant coffee granules
- 1 tablespoon hot water
- 1/2 cup heavy cream
- 2 cups heavy cream, divided
- 3 large eggs, separated
- 1/4 cup granulated sugar
- 1 teaspoon vanilla extract
- 1/4 teaspoon salt
- Cocoa powder or chocolate shavings for garnish (optional)

Instructions:

1. PREPARE THE CRUST:

1. Preheat your oven to 350°F (175°C).
2. In a bowl, mix together the chocolate cookie crumbs and melted butter until well combined.
3. Press the mixture into the bottom of a 9-inch springform pan.

4. Bake the crust for 8-10 minutes, then remove from the oven and let it cool completely.

2. MAKE THE CHOCOLATE MOCHA MOUSSE:

1. In a small bowl, dissolve the instant coffee granules in hot water. Let it cool.
2. In a heatproof bowl, combine the semi-sweet chocolate chips and 1/2 cup of heavy cream.
3. Place the bowl over a pot of simmering water (double boiler) and stir until the chocolate is melted and the mixture is smooth.
4. Remove from heat and let it cool slightly.
5. In a separate bowl, whip 1 cup of heavy cream until stiff peaks form. Set aside.
6. In another bowl, beat the egg yolks with granulated sugar until thick and pale yellow in color. Stir in the vanilla extract.
7. Gradually stir the cooled coffee mixture into the egg yolk mixture until well combined.
8. Gradually stir the cooled chocolate mixture into the egg yolk mixture until well combined.
9. Gently fold the whipped cream into the chocolate mocha mixture until no streaks remain. Set aside.

3. ASSEMBLE THE CAKE:

1. In a clean, dry bowl, beat the egg whites with salt until stiff peaks form.
2. Gently fold the beaten egg whites into the chocolate mocha mousse mixture until evenly combined.
3. Pour the mousse over the cooled crust in the springform pan.
4. Smooth the top with a spatula, then refrigerate the cake for at least 4 hours or until set.

4. SERVE:

1. Once the mousse has set, carefully remove the sides of the springform pan.
2. Garnish with cocoa powder or chocolate shavings if desired.
3. Slice and serve chilled. Enjoy your Sinful Chocolate Mocha Mousse Cake!

Dreamy Chocolate Orange Mousse Cake Recipe

Ingredients:

- 1 1/2 cups chocolate cookie crumbs
- 1/4 cup unsalted butter, melted
- 2 cups semi-sweet chocolate chips
- 1 tablespoon orange zest
- 1/2 cup orange juice
- 1/2 cup heavy cream
- 2 cups heavy cream, divided
- 3 large eggs, separated
- 1/4 cup granulated sugar
- 1 teaspoon vanilla extract
- 1/4 teaspoon salt
- Additional whipped cream and orange zest for garnish (optional)

Instructions:

1. PREPARE THE CRUST:

1. Preheat your oven to 350°F (175°C).
2. In a bowl, mix together the chocolate cookie crumbs and melted butter until well combined.
3. Press the mixture into the bottom of a 9-inch springform pan.

4. Bake the crust for 8-10 minutes, then remove from the oven and let it cool completely.

2. MAKE THE CHOCOLATE ORANGE MOUSSE:

1. In a small saucepan, heat the orange juice and orange zest until just simmering. Let it cool.
2. In a heatproof bowl, combine the semi-sweet chocolate chips and 1/2 cup of heavy cream.
3. Place the bowl over a pot of simmering water (double boiler) and stir until the chocolate is melted and the mixture is smooth.
4. Remove from heat and let it cool slightly.
5. In a separate bowl, whip 1 cup of heavy cream until stiff peaks form. Set aside.
6. In another bowl, beat the egg yolks with granulated sugar until thick and pale yellow in color. Stir in the vanilla extract.
7. Gradually stir the cooled orange mixture into the egg yolk mixture until well combined.
8. Gradually stir the cooled chocolate mixture into the egg yolk mixture until well combined.
9. Gently fold the whipped cream into the chocolate orange mixture until no streaks remain. Set aside.

3. ASSEMBLE THE CAKE:

1. In a clean, dry bowl, beat the egg whites with salt until stiff peaks form.
2. Gently fold the beaten egg whites into the chocolate orange mousse mixture until evenly combined.
3. Pour the mousse over the cooled crust in the springform pan.
4. Smooth the top with a spatula, then refrigerate the cake for at least 4 hours or until set.

4. SERVE:

1. Once the mousse has set, carefully remove the sides of the springform pan.
2. Garnish with whipped cream and additional orange zest if desired.
3. Slice and serve chilled. Enjoy your Dreamy Chocolate Orange Mousse Cake!

Made in United States
Troutdale, OR
04/21/2024

19336548R00046